THE OCEANS EXPLORED

OCEAN POLLUTION

Claudia Martin

Illustrated by Fiona Osbaldstone

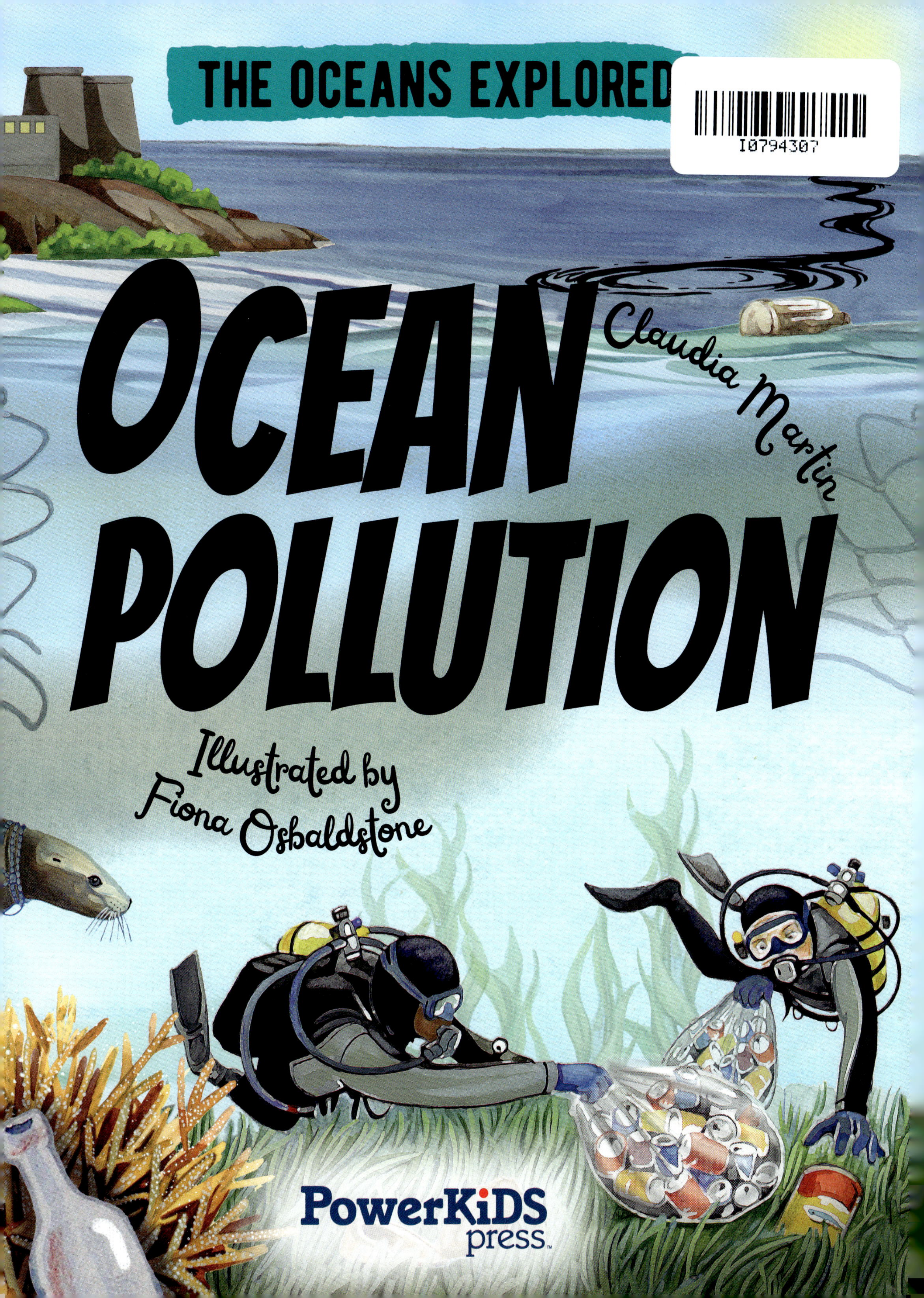

PowerKiDS press

I0794307

Published in 2026
by The Rosen Publishing Group, Inc.
2544 Clinton Street, Buffalo, NY 14224

First published in 2021 in Great Britain by Wayland

Copyright © Hodder and Stoughton 2021

Credits

Author and editor: Claudia Martin
Illustrator: Fiona Osbaldstone
Designer: Dan Prescott, Couper Street Type Co.
Proofreader: Annabel Savery

The publisher would like to thank the following for permission to reproduce their photographs:
Alamy: Paulo Oliveira 4l and 20, Imagedoc 5b, Helmut Corneli 9, Arterra Picture Library 10, Tim Cuff 23, Jeff Rotman 24, Debra Behr 27; Getty Images: Martin Harvey/The Image Bank 7, roclwyr/iStock 28; Shutterstock: steve estvanik 4r, FloridaStock 5tl, Narongsak Nagadhana 5tr, Nicole Helgason 13, hans engbers 15, Photography by Kader Kurt 16, Andrea Izzotti 19.

Every attempt has been made to clear copyright. Should there be any inadvertent omission please apply to the publisher for rectification.

The website addresses (URLs) included in this book were valid at the time of going to press. However, it is possible that contents or addresses may have changed since the publication of this book. No responsibility for any such changes can be accepted by either the author or the Publisher.

Cataloging-in-Publication Data

Names: Martin, Claudia, author. | Osbaldstone, Fiona, illustrator.
Title: Ocean pollution / by Claudia Martin, illustrated by Fiona Osbaldstone.
Description: Buffalo, NY : PowerKids Press, 2026. | Series: The oceans explored | Includes glossary and index.
Identifiers: ISBN 9781499454031 (pbk.) | ISBN 9781499454048 (library bound) | ISBN 9781499454055 (ebook)
Subjects: LCSH: Marine pollution--Juvenile literature | .Ocean--Juvenile literature.
Classification: LCC GC1090.M378 2026 | DDC 393.739'409162--dc23

All rights reserved.

No part of this book may be reproduced in any form without permission in writing from the publisher, except by a reviewer.

Manufactured in the United States of America

CPSIA Compliance Information: Batch #CSPK26. For further information contact Rosen Publishing at 1-800-237-9932.

Find us on

CONTENTS

OCEAN POLLUTION

The world's oceans are at risk from pollution. Pollution is anything that harms the water or its animals and plants. Humans pollute the oceans by drilling for fuels, burning fossil fuels, releasing waste, building on the coast, and disturbing animals. Pollution has put more than 2,000 ocean animals at risk of extinction.

RELEASING WASTE

Waste from toilets, farms, factories, and homes can end up in the oceans.

DISTURBING ANIMALS

Noise and light from ships, drilling, coastal cities, and hotels can confuse animals.

BURNING FOSSIL FUELS

Oil, natural gas, and coal are called fossil fuels. When they are burned, they let out gases that trap the Sun's heat. Slowly, the oceans are warming and sea ice is melting.

DRILLING FOR FUELS

The fuels oil and natural gas can be pumped from beneath the seabed, but care must be taken not to leak them into the water.

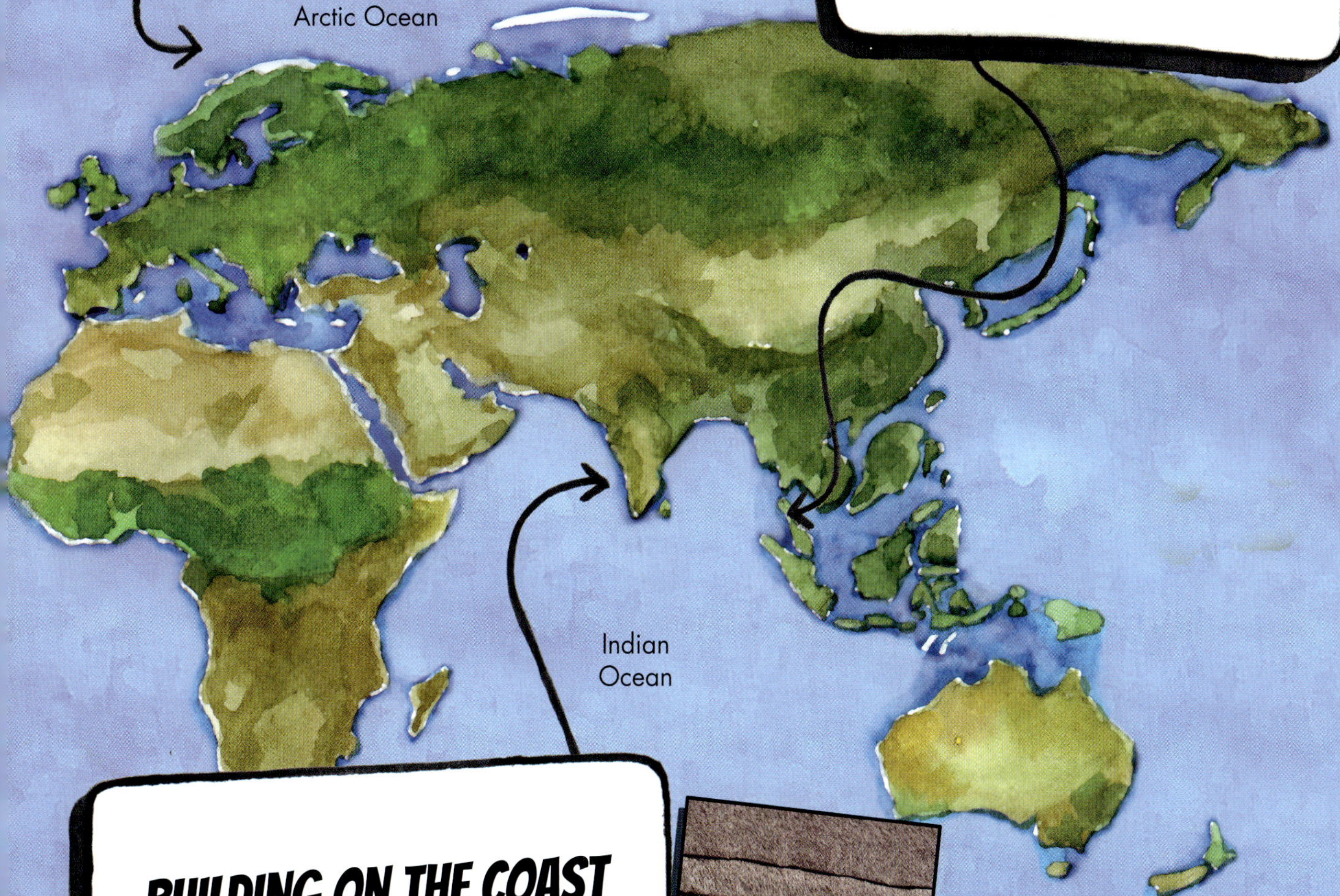

BUILDING ON THE COAST

When hotels, factories, and cities are built on the coast, they can destroy the habitats of seabirds and other creatures.

DRILLING FOR OIL AND GAS

Oil and natural gas are fuels that are burned to make heat or electricity.

In places such as the Persian Gulf, in the Indian Ocean, these fuels are found under the seafloor.

When scientists find oil and gas beneath the ocean, structures called oil rigs are built, often with long legs fixed to the seafloor. Drills are used to make a hole in the seafloor, then the fuel is pumped out. Seafloor animals, such as flatfish and crabs, find their homes criss-crossed by pipes, while they may be disturbed by noise and mess.

Oil is taken to land by pipes or by ships called tankers. Occasionally, a pipe or an oil tanker leaks. These oil spills can kill plants, such as seagrasses, which in turn harms all the animals that eat the plants or hide among them. When oil coats the feathers of seabirds, they find it hard to fly and float. Today, laws tell oil companies to take care of the oceans and do everything they can to avoid oil spills.

A Cape penguin is covered in oil leaked from a tanker, on the coast of southern Africa.

RISING TEMPERATURES

The Earth's air, land, and oceans are growing slowly warmer.

Hotter water is damaging coral reefs, endangering reef-living fish and other animals.

When fossil fuels are burned in car engines, factories, and homes, they release carbon dioxide and other gases. These gases trap the Sun's heat around Earth. If we keep burning lots of fossil fuels, the oceans may be 7°F (4°C) hotter by the end of this century.

Many corals, such as staghorn coral, get much of their food from tiny algae that live inside their bodies. The algae make food from sunlight. When seawater gets too warm, the coral reacts and pushes out the algae, making the coral look paler. This is called bleaching (shown on the right). Without algae, the coral begins to starve. It can recover if the ocean temperature returns to normal.

On the coast of Fiji, in the Pacific Ocean, staghorn coral has been bleached by rising sea temperatures.

A walrus rests on the sea ice before diving once more into the chilly Arctic Ocean.

MELTING ICE

Ice covers parts of the Arctic Ocean, as well as the Southern Ocean around Antarctica.

As the air and oceans warm, this sea ice is melting.

By the end of this century, there may be no ice on the Arctic Ocean in summer. Year after year, there is less ice than before. This is putting in danger all the animals that live on the sea ice, such as polar bears and walruses in the Arctic, and Adélie penguins and Weddell seals in the Antarctic.

Walruses need to climb onto sea ice to have babies. As the sea ice melts and grows smaller, many walruses are swimming long distances to reach dry land to give birth. This means they are farther from the shelled sea creatures they eat. This puts walrus babies at risk, as their mothers must leave them for longer periods to find food.

ACIDIC OCEAN

Burning fossil fuels has put too much carbon dioxide into the air.

The world's oceans are soaking up lots of the extra carbon dioxide.

When too much carbon dioxide mixes with seawater, the water becomes slightly acidic. An acid can wear away some materials. Acidic ocean water is, little by little, wearing away the shells and skeletons of sea creatures, such as snails, clams, oysters, and spiky sea urchins. They have to work extra hard to maintain their shells, which is stopping them putting effort into making babies. Over time, this could make them go extinct.

Today, many countries are trying to burn fewer fossil fuels by using other sources of energy, such as the wind or sunlight. Rather than burning oil in car engines, more people are driving electric cars or using engine fuels made from plants, such as sugar cane.

Off the Atlantic coast of Honduras, a scientist measures the growth of black long-spined sea urchins.

SEWAGE

Sewage is the waste from toilets, as well as from baths and dishwashers.

Many countries get rid of their sewage safely, but some waste ends up in the ocean.

One of the world's wealthiest countries, Canada, has sewage treatment plants where waste is cleaned. However, some untreated Canadian sewage is still carried by pipes to the Atlantic and Pacific Oceans. In some countries, such as India, a lot of people do not have a toilet. Some of their waste is carried into the Indian Ocean by rivers.

Sewage carries disease, soaps, and medicines. These can cause illness in the sea creatures that live near coasts, as well as the bigger animals that eat them. Oysters cling to rocks along the coast, where they can suck up disease-causing bacteria along with their food. When people collect these oysters to eat, the oysters can make them very sick.

A sewage pipe discharges its waste into the warm shallows of a Philippine beach, in the western Pacific Ocean.

Fringing Australia's Balmoral Beach is an algae bloom known as a red tide.

FARMING

When it rains, chemicals used on farmland can be washed into rivers.

The rivers carry the chemicals to the ocean, where they do great harm.

Across the world, many farmers use chemicals called fertilizers on fields. Fertilizers give the soil extra nutrients, which are substances that make plants grow well. When these nutrients reach the ocean, they are food for tiny algae. The extra food makes the algae grow out of control, sometimes filling the water with algae blooms.

Some algae, such as the red *Karenia*, release poisons into the water. Large blooms can kill dolphins, turtles, and seabirds. Blooms also use up the water's oxygen. Without enough oxygen to absorb, lots of fish can die. To help stop algae blooms, many farmers try to use less fertilizer.

INDUSTRIAL WASTE

Industrial waste is the leftover materials from factories, mills, and mines.

If this waste gets into the ocean it can enter food chains, which are series of living things that feed on each other.

Industrial waste includes chemicals, oil, and metal from factories. Paper mills, which turn wood into paper, leave behind paper mush, while mines make heaps of gravel. In many countries, laws make sure that waste is recycled or carefully thrown away. Yet some waste is still dumped in the ocean or carried there by rivers or pipes.

The Atlantic Ocean contains too much mercury, a poisonous metal from factory waste. Plants and algae that have soaked up mercury are eaten by small fish, which are eaten by seabirds, bigger fish, or humans. Mercury can damage the brain of every animal in the food chain.

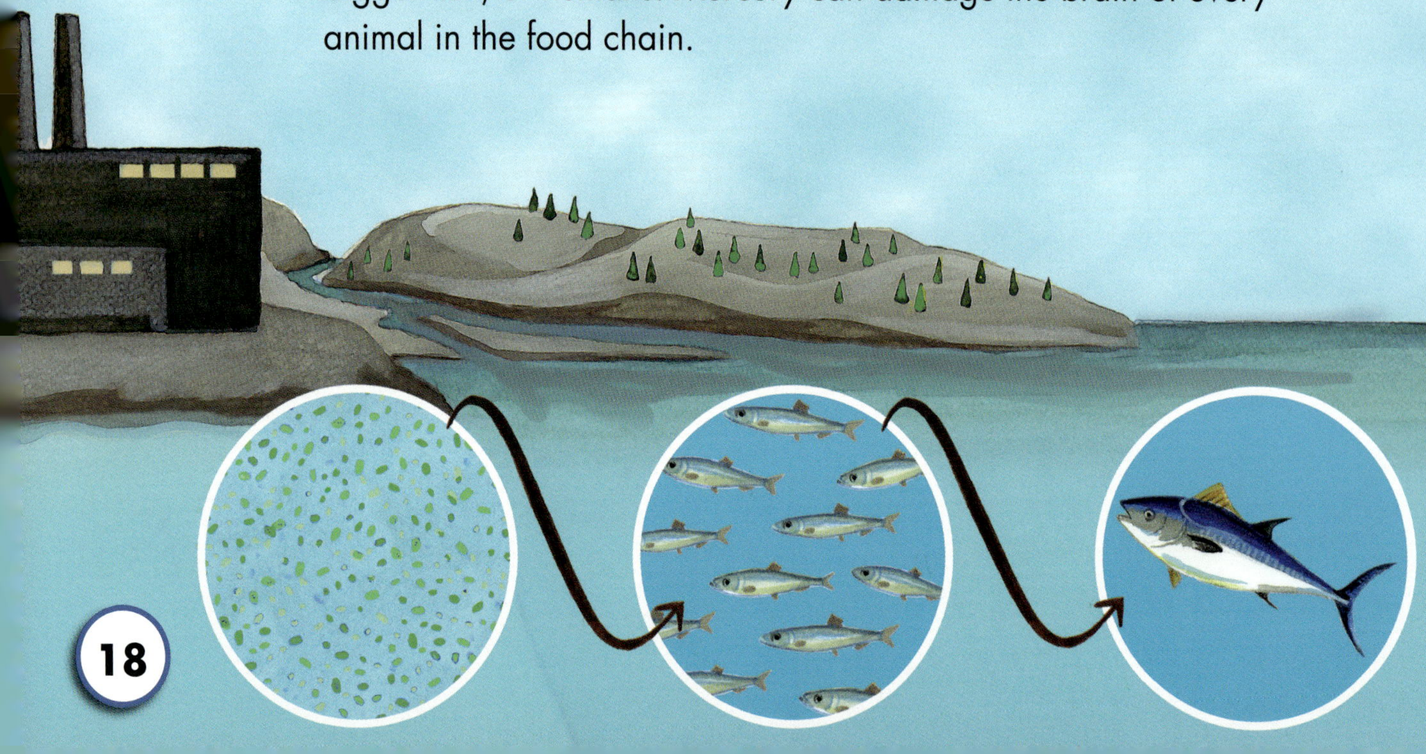

Watching for the right moment to strike, a striped marlin herds together a shoal of sardines.

A common bottlenose dolphin plays with a plastic six pack, made to hold together cans of fizzy drinks.

PLASTIC

Some people throw plastic trash, from bags to bottles, into the oceans.

Since plastic takes up to 500 years to break down, the water is filled with more and more.

Scientists think there are 110 million tons (100 million mt) of plastic in the oceans, which is about the weight of 100 million cars. Many ocean animals, including seals, dolphins, and birds, can have trouble breathing if they swallow plastic items or get them wrapped around their throat.

In the North Pacific Ocean, huge amounts of plastic have been driven together by moving streams of water, called currents. This area, known as the Great Pacific Garbage Patch, is about the same size as France. Seabirds, such as the Laysan albatross, mistake the plastic for food and even feed it to their chicks.

MAKING A NOISE

Ship engines, underwater mining, and oil drilling are making the oceans noisier.

This is disturbing animals that use their hearing to find food and their way.

Under water, sound travels far better than light, so hearing is usually more important than sight for sea animals. In the dark of the deep sea, some fish cannot see at all. Human noise disturbs the water, stopping these fish from feeling the ripples made by moving prey.

Dolphins and some whales, such as sperm and beluga whales, use sounds to find their way. They make clicking noises, which bounce off objects and return to them. The speed of the returning echoes lets them map their surroundings. If there is too much noise, these animals can get lost and become stuck on beaches, where they need to be rescued.

Scientists rescue a group of pilot whales that have become stuck on a beach in New Zealand.

In the Pacific Ocean's Sea of Cortez, a thresher shark has been entangled in a forgotten fishing net.

CARELESS FISHING

When humans catch only the fish we can eat, we do no harm to the oceans.

Yet when fishing is done thoughtlessly, animals and habitats are put at risk.

Sometimes fishing nets are lost or left behind in the water. These can trap ocean animals, stopping them from finding food. If the animals need to swim to the surface to breathe air, they can drown. Every year, turtles, dolphins, whales, seals, and birds die for this reason.

In some fishing communities, fishermen set off explosives in the water, killing or stunning many fish so they can be collected easily. As well as being very dangerous for the fishermen, the explosions destroy coral reefs. Once the reefs are damaged, all the animals that live among the coral may die too.

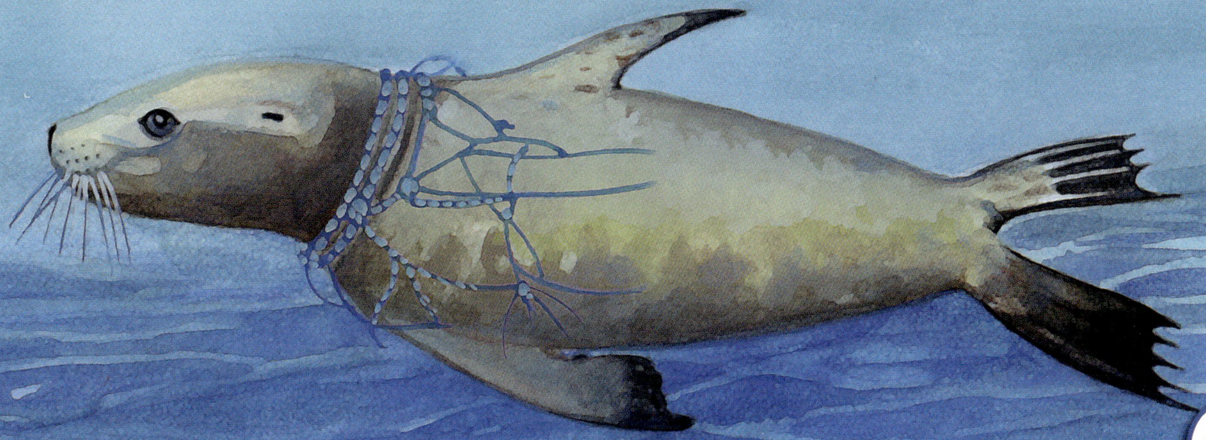

CHANGING COASTS

People build towns, factories, and hotels along coasts.

They cover sand, mud, and grass with stone, metal, and concrete.

Building along the coast can disturb the resting places of seals and sea lions. Plants that live in shallow water along the coast, such as mangrove trees, seagrasses, and rushes, may be uprooted, struck by boats, or poisoned by chemicals.

Sea animals that lay their eggs on land, such as turtles and seabirds, may find their nesting spots disturbed. Sea turtles lay their eggs in holes they dig on sandy beaches around the Indian, Atlantic, and Pacific Oceans. If tourists push beach umbrellas into the sand, they damage the eggs. When the eggs hatch, the babies must find their way to the sea. If they are confused by noise and lights from hotels and towns, they can get lost.

Tourists gaze at green turtles on a beach in Hawaii, in the Pacific Ocean.

A sea otter naps in a kelp forest, holding the kelp to prevent itself from drifting out to sea.

CLEANING UP

Across the world, people are working together to save the oceans.

Laws are made to stop pollution, while people clean up waste and rescue sea animals.

By 1992, Monterey Bay in the United States, in the Pacific Ocean, was polluted by waste from factories. The bay is home to a kelp forest, where many of these large plant-like algae grow from the seabed. The kelp were dying.

Environmentalists, charities, and ordinary people persuaded the government to make the area a sanctuary, protected by law. Pollution and drilling for oil were forbidden. Today, the kelp forest has regrown and is home to kelp bass, sea otters, and leopard sharks. An aquarium helps visitors to understand the bay's habitat. It also teaches what we can all do to save the oceans: make fewer car trips, use less plastic, reuse and recycle our waste, and join charities that protect the oceans.

GLOSSARY

acidic able to wear away some materials

algae simple, plant-like living things

algae bloom a large growth of algae in water

bacteria tiny living things that can sometimes cause disease

bay a part of the coast where the land curves inward

carbon dioxide a gas that is found naturally in the air and is also released by burning the fuels oil, gas, and coal

chemical a human-made substance

coal a solid fuel found in the ground

coral reef a stony underwater ridge made of the skeletons of millions of tiny animals called coral polyps

energy power that can provide light and heat or run machines

environmentalist a person who works to protect the natural world

extinction the death of the last living animal of a particular type

fertilizer a substance added to the soil to make plants grow large and fast

fossil fuel a fuel formed over millions of years from the bodies of dead plants and animals

fuel a material that is burned to make heat

habitat the natural home of a group of animals and plants

industrial released by, or made in, factories, mines, and mills

mangrove tree a tree that grows in warm, shallow seawater

natural gas a mixture of gases that is found inside Earth's rocks and can be burned as a fuel

oil a liquid fuel found inside Earth's rocks

oil spill the accidental release of oil into water

oxygen a gas, found in the air, that animals need to live

plastic a human-made material made from fossil fuels

pollution releasing harmful materials or energy into the ocean, air, or soil

prey an animal that is eaten by other animals

sanctuary an area that is protected for plants and animals

seagrass a grass-like plant that grows from the seabed

sea ice ice that forms on the ocean around the poles

sewage treatment plant a place where sewage is cleaned

waste unwanted materials

FURTHER READING

Books

Climate Change (Ecographics), Izzi Howell (Franklin Watts, 2019)

Endangered Wildlife: Ocean Life, Anita Ganeri (Wayland, 2020)

Oceans in Danger, Alicia Green (Children's Press, 2025)

Plastic Planet: How Plastic Came to Rule the World, Georgia Amson-Bradshaw (Franklin Watts, 2020)

Websites

Find out more about saving the ocean from pollution on these websites:

https://climatekids.nasa.gov/climate-change-meaning

https://plasticoceans.org

www.mcsuk.org

wwf.panda.org/our_work/oceans

INDEX